Let Me Re-Introduce Myself

You Don't Know The Cost

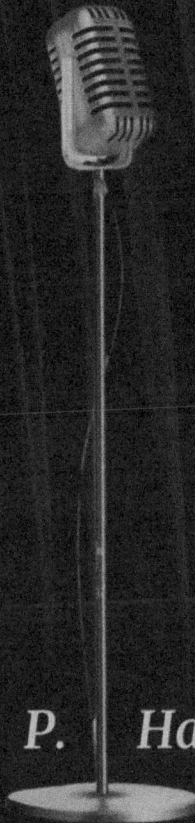

Kenyatta P. Hardaway

LET ME
RE-INTRODUCE
MYSELF

YOU DON'T KNOW THE COST

KENYATTA P. HARDAWAY

KAIROS
EDITING & PUBLISHING

California   Missouri

KAIROS
EDITING & PUBLISHING

Published by
KAIROS Editing & Publishing, LLC
Oceanside, CA/ Sikeston, MO
kairosagent72@gmail.com

Editor: Dr. Karen D. Lomax
Cover design: Dr. Karen D. Lomax

Scripture quotations are KJV unless otherwise
marked.

DEDICATION

This book is dedicated back to my Lord and Savior, Jesus Christ.

To my children: I thank God for choosing me to mommy you. I would like to thank everyone for your love, support, and constant prayers.

TABLE OF CONTENTS

INTRODUCTION

In May of 2020, God asked me who I was in Him & it made me realize that I am more than a conqueror. Believing that I could do all things through Him because He has given me the strength to do so, to carry out His purpose & plan for my life. I was given a 19 day assignment to re-introduce myself & in those days it allowed me to grow a stronger & an intimate relationship with the Lord, & that is how the Re-Introduce Yourself Ministry was born! Connecting jumping rope to the ministry was huge for me; it reminded me of my relationship with Him. I see it as God at one end of the rope & me at the other end & if I stay connected to God I will not separate from Him, but when I start to depart from Him my rope starts to split in half which causes me to be further & further away from God. *Let Me Re-Introduce Myself* is the introduction to another extensive writing project that is currently in the works. This book is my testimony of how I came to recognize that God will untie the kinks and knots in my life as long if I stay connected to Him at all times. Don't get me wrong there are still many kinks and knots in my life that God has to still deliver me from and I'm okay with that. I am more than a conqueror. I can do all things through Christ who strengthens me and so can you too!

~Kenyatta

MY DECLARATION

Let me introduce myself!

My name is Kenyatta.

I am a mother of three amazing children.

I am a grandmother to one joyful

grandson.

I am a Certified Christian life coach.

I am a personal witness of Christ Jesus

(Acts 1:8)

I am a Christian Lady Boss!

YOU DON'T KNOW THE COST

You don't know the cost of my praise and what I had to go through to get where I am today. When I was young, my dad ended up going to prison, and my mom began dating a man who was very abusive and controlling. My innocence was taken away by him, and I had to watch him constantly abuse my mom.

At the age of eight, my mom was murdered by this abuser, and I became motherless. My brother, sister, and I were thankfully adopted by my grandma so we could stay together. We would have otherwise been awarded custody to the state and separated, going to different foster homes. My family was blessed with a wonderful social worker who used to visit us and helped in so many ways. She inspired me to become a social worker when I grew up to help moms get their children back. Although I did not become a licensed social worker, my job right now requires many aspects of social work, and I am able to help mothers and children every day.

My innocence was once again taken away from me later on in my life when I was molested by a family member that I trusted. These events had a huge effect on me, yet I placed my mom's murder and being abused in the back of my head, never to be thought of again. It wasn't until later in my adult life that God opened my eyes to see that I had to go through this so that I could become who I am today. He helped me realize that the things I went through weren't just for me, but for everyone in the battle right now that needs hope and encouragement to get out of the struggles they are in.

I remember one particular incident when my mom was making rice, and she always cut me a small square slice of butter and placed it on top of my rice. I would eat my butter first, and my abuser would get so mad at me for doing so. One day he got so angry and yelled at me for doing it. My mom tried defending me and he yelled at her because she was defending me.

I was put in the closet with no food because he thought I was playing with my food. I remember peeking out of the closet and he was fighting my mom. He made her take off all her clothes and he beat her with a belt mainly using the buckle. The door squeaked a little and he stopped hitting her. She turned around to me with a huge smile on her face, but....I could tell that she was in pain from being hit constantly. She said, "Key-Key it's okay go back in the closet, Mama is ok." She would always tell me that it's ok and smile. Knowing in my little brain that it really wasn't ok, I didn't know how to protect my mom. My sister was able to get away to go call my grandma (my dad's mom) to come to get us. I thank God for my sister knowing my grandma's phone number to free us from this abuser. I truly thank God for my sister even more today.

Whenever the Social Worker would visit, I was always told to go back into the room to play. I was never allowed to share my side of the story of what my mom's abuser did to me. I know my family felt that I was too young and didn't understand, or what was happening until I wrote a letter to the Social Worker and told her everything I remembered. She promised to never tell anyone what I had shared with her.

THE MARRIAGE

On May 17, 1997, I married my children's father. Going into a marriage without God or counseling was very hard. There were times when I didn't want my husband to touch or hug me because it made me feel as if I were back in that closet as a little girl. I felt smothered, I felt like I was being raped all over again by both my mom's abuser and the family member. My past played a huge part on an intimate level.

When my children were born, their playing affected me as well, and when they would fight, wrestle or argue, it would trigger something inside of me. Thinking that they would hurt each other, I would yell out, "STOP!!" But all along they were only playing. My heart would race and pump so hard it felt like I was having a heart attack; I would become sweaty and my head would spin. All of this would happen suddenly

THE DIAGNOSIS

When I tell you that God's grace and His mercy is upon your life, please believe it, because I didn't have the strong intimate relationship that I have now. I thought I heard the man who molested me. I didn't realize I was battling the enemy in my mind. God spared my life that day! I ended up being admitted to the fifth floor of Regions Hospital. The nurses were telling the staff to turn off the television so I wouldn't see what was going on.

I didn't even know that the World Trade Center had planes flown into it. The staff and nurses assumed I was affected by and that it may cause me to have another panic attack. The social worker asked me why I was there; at that point, she was the fifth person to ask, and

I had to retell my whole day over. When I told her that the guy who murdered my mom wanted me to crash my car, she assumed I was talking about the crash of the planes that crashed into the World Trade Centers. The entire day was stressful and retelling my story was stressful. After seeing a therapist and various doctors, they diagnosed me with post-traumatic stress disorder (PTSD) and depression.

September 11, 2001, was a very trying time for me. I was about five and a half months pregnant and it was about 3:00 p.m. I was driving in my car alone on a summer afternoon, listening to my gospel music, when I began to hear a voice in my head. This voice was telling me, "Crash your car! Nobody loves you, so you might as well go ahead and crash your car!" I looked around as if someone else was in the car because the voice was so vivid. Before I knew it, I heard the voice again, telling me, "Crash your car!" It felt like I was going crazy, so I turned my radio down as I went across Dale Street. I heard it again, "Crash your car!" At this point, I didn't know the Holy Spirit as I know Him now, but I now know my heavenly Father lead me to safety.

All I remember is driving to a place called *Chrysalis for Women,* and I sped into the place and left my driver-side door open. I ran in yelling, crying, and screaming, "The man that murdered my mom told me to crash my car!" The women inside were panicking because I was in such frenzy, and they thought he was coming in behind me. They didn't know that the man who murdered my mom had already passed on three years prior. They were able to calm me down and help me take some deep breaths so I could explain what was happening. I told them I felt like hurting myself because that's what the voice was telling me.

We need to understand that mental health is a real battle in and of itself. Everything that was done to me in my past was coming back to me-- reliving the molestation and sexual abuse, the scenes from seeing my mother lying in a casket, flashbacks of being put in a closet without food, and watching my mom being beaten on and disrespected. That was the moment I realized I couldn't do anything but call on a God with whom I had no relationship. Because of His grace upon my life, and the love that He has for me, He heard my cry and my plea. I was placed on a seventy-two-hour hold and then released.

"re"

{prefix}

Again

Anew

I REFUSE TO LET THIS HAPPEN TO ME

I have been dealing with depression and PTSD for the majority of my adult life, which has been a struggle for me. There was a point where I would go into a store and BOOM my PTSD kicked in---I would hear voices that sounded like my mother's abuser, and I would then fly out of the store thinking he was in there to get me, forgetting at that moment that he had already passed away. I would have dreams that he was coming to murder me. I would see other men that resembled him, and I would have panic attacks to the point where I had to be hospitalized because I felt like these thoughts of suicide were becoming too much. I wanted to end my life.

I remember trying to juggle being a mom, wife and keeping my sanity-- how do you do that?! I was in the process of getting in right standing with God. I knew that I was tired and needed healing. This abusive man was affecting me and he wasn't even alive! To top it all off, I was having random seizures. I was hospitalized for a week to have tests done on my brain to see why I was having these seizures.

After running several tests, they concluded that I had something called, "pseudo seizures" which look like epileptic seizures but are not epileptic. Thank God, I didn't have epilepsy, but, these pseudo seizures were starting to take over my life and this demon was trying to control who I was in Christ. I refused to allow this to happen to me--I got the therapy and counseling that I needed to help me get through it, but I know that God's compassion and love over my life is what healed and saved me!

🎙 THE BATTLE ROOM

God placed it in my heart to create a prayer closet. I call it my "Battle Room." It's where I go to pray and talk to God. I often go into my prayer closet to meditate and sometimes just to cry. The backstory to this is, when I was younger my mom's abuser would use the closet as a form of punishment, so--- I didn't like closets growing up. It was traumatic to me, but looks how Romans 8:28 played a part in this entire thing: *"All things work together for the good of those who love God and are called according to His purpose."* I now use the closet that was used to punish me as a place where I can go and pray, praise, and worship. It was a battle room for punishment, but now it's a "battle room" for God's glory.

God: "Wake up! Wake up, daughter! Good morning, meet me in the Battle Room!"

Me: "Good Morning Lord, Lord I thank you for waking me up this morning."

My Battle Room is the name God gave me for my prayer closet. One morning, as I entered the room at about 6:00 a.m., I began to say to the Lord, "Lord, forgive me for anything that I have said or done that was not pleasing to your sight or to your ears. Asking God for forgiveness is what I do before asking Him for anything. Lord, who is it that You would want me to help today?" The Lord began to ask me, "Who am I in you?" I had never heard Him ask me this question before.

At that time, I didn't have an answer for Him. I then said to the Lord, "Lord, to be honest, I don't quite know who I am in you anymore, but I am about to head out to work and as soon as I return Lord, I will have an answer." The best part of waking up is...well you know the rest of the commercial, but that day waking up meant realizing that for me to know who I was in Christ, I had to know who He was.

🎙 THE ANSWER

It was a typical busy workday and I just couldn't seem to get out of my mind what the Lord had asked of me. By mid-day, as I began to set my mind on things above and think about the question that God had asked me, I began to think about who I was in Him. I started telling myself that "I am more than a conqueror," then I began to say "Greater is He that's in me than he that's in the world..." I went on and on to say, "I can do all things through Christ that strengthens me."

Knowing these things gave me hope and a little more encouragement. Just knowing that I already had what it took because in Him I do live, move and have my being. At this point, it was about 5:00 p.m., the end of my shift. I couldn't wait to get home and back into the

Battle Room to tell God what I had come up with. Though I could have just told Him right there, sitting at my desk, something miraculous often happens in my Battle Room. I got home and started talking to the Lord, telling Him who I was in Him and I started hearing the Lord say to me, "Daughter (that's what He calls me). Daughter, re-introduce yourself."

When I heard Him say this to me, I instantly felt a breakthrough in my spirit. I felt this sense of peace; it almost felt like at that moment, God wanted me to see me as He saw me. Recognizing that I was more than I thought I was, especially being told by others that I would be nothing when I grew up. Growing up and being told that God didn't call me into His ministry, or my visions of what I hear and see are just a coincidence or Deja Vu. Hearing these things in my life made me think I wasn't worth

anything. But, God knew who I was in Him

GET INSPIRED

I had been following a lady on Facebook and she started a Jump Rope Challenge. I thought I would at least consider it. So I began to watch her--she would go outside every day-- rain or shine, and she would jump. Each day was a different number. I felt so inspired and she encouraged me daily, but I would always just watch her instead of joining her.

Finally, one day, I realized that I was starting to gain weight and wasn't very active. I even began to lose my breath going up and down the stairs in my home. That's when I knew I had to do something. I went to purchase a jump rope at Walmart in May 2020, and I went to the park with my daughter and nephew. When I began to jump, thinking that I would be able to do twenty-five jumps and when I reached fifteen, I was very much out of breath and wanted to give up. But I began to tell myself, "I can do all things through Christ who strengthens me." (Philippians 4:13). I kept repeating that, knowing that I needed God's strength to reach my goal of twenty-five jumps. My resiliency kicked in and I had to keep going. I trusted in myself and with the Lord's help, was able to accomplish my goal of twenty-five. I was so proud of myself.

THE INSTRUCTIONS

The next morning I woke up and proceeded back downstairs to my Battle Room. On this particular morning, the Lord had given me specific instructions for nineteen days, to go live on Facebook and "Re-Introduce" myself. I said, "Lord, I haven't studied and I don't know what to say." I never really liked to go live on Facebook or any social media platform. At this particular time, I just basically ignored the fact that God had spoken this to me, and because of fear, I didn't want to do it. The Bible says that obedience is better than sacrifice. But, did I want to risk the sacrifice?

It was the year of Covid-19.; I was in perfectly good health. I went into work feeling fine, but by the end of the day, I began to feel sick and burning up with a high fever and body aches. I was feeling so horrible that night; I ended up calling my supervisor and telling her that I didn't think I would make it to work the next day. By the next afternoon, as I began to pray over myself and speak of healing over my entire body, by the grace of God, I started to feel better. I was told by my director to get a Covid test, which I did. When Covid-19 first hit, there were a few days for test results and fourteen-day quarantine.

I had no choice but to be home and do just what God had instructed me to do. I had no excuse not to do what God told me. I was more so afraid of going live on Facebook because people that I knew and didn't know would be watching me. But, my test came back negative, and God began to remind me of the story of Jeremiah; when God told him to go and "Do not be afraid of their faces, for I am with you to deliver you," says the Lord. So I said, "Okay Lord, I am completely depending on you to lead me through this nineteen-day journey!

CONNECT THE ROPE

God gave me this awesome revelation as I was jumping rope. I created a calendar with one of my cousins and on each day of the month was a different number that I had to jump. I started to think about the connection that we all need to have with God. I began looking at this challenge as if God was on one end of the rope and I was on the other end.

As I jumped, it made me think of the connection between Him and me; knowing that on this jumping journey, I can do it with His strength. I can depend on God to see me through. I also thought, "Well, if I keep sinning this would get me further and further away from God. The rope 'connection' would start to separate me from God, but we must know that nothing shall separate me from the Love of God,

not even sin.

The Journey Begins

Who are you in Christ? In Psalm 139:14, God begins to speak and say, "You are not who you used to be. I have redeemed you, I have set you free. Stop limiting who you are in me and stop minimizing who I called you to be. If I called you to minister, be the best minister that you can be; leading, guiding people back to Christ, encouraging people, being an effective witness for those who are lost." He begins to say, "People will know you by your fruit." The way you carry yourself and the way you love God's people. You are who God says that you are. You are more than a conqueror. "...*Greater is He that's in you, than he that's in the world*" (1John 4:4, para). God is great in you, so you are destined to be great!

WHAT GIVES MY LIFE MEANING

What gives my life meaning? Connecting with and building a relationship with Him. I was born to worship! No matter my ups, downs, fears, or failures or having a reason to live. My children give me a reason to live. There were times where I wanted to end my life feeling like I wasn't loved and I was losing my identity. The moment God saved me was when I realized that with God my life is worth more.

HOW TO SHUT UP THE NAYSAYERS UP
IN JESUS NAME

1 Peter 2:15 --Tell us how to do so....you shut the "naysayers" up by continuing to do the work of the Lord. I often worry about what people think of me and how they would perceive me. Many people will judge you and call you every name in the book, especially if you are now walking upright with the Lord. Continue to be an effective witness for God. Keep walking, fighting, building, learning, and serving.

WHAT I HAVE LEARNED ALONG THE WAY

Because of your faith, not even a whisper can affect your determination. God said He discharges, and I learned to put him first faith comes by hearing. We all should be going through drastic measures to meet Jesus or to seek Jesus.

What are the 3 biggest things I've learned in life?

Trust-Proverbs 3:5-6 *"Trust in the Lord with all your heart, lean not unto your own understanding, but in all your ways acknowledge Him and He will direct your path."* I trust God with everything that's inside of me, knowing that I can't do anything without Him. Even with the things that I don't understand, I seek Him for the answers. I have learned to acknowledge Him and trust that He will direct me in the direction that I need to go.

Faith. -The Bible declares that we ought to have faith *the size of a mustard seed.* When I thought about this, all I could think was, "I can move something huge with a small piece of faith?" I can move obstacles if I just let God do it and know that He can, believing in the substance of things hoped for and the evidence of things unseen. I had to learn that even when I didn't see it, even when I didn't think I was hearing from God, I had to continue to have this thing called a "consistent faith."

Forgiveness. -I've learned that holding onto something can kill you! That's exactly what the enemy wants to do: destroy you, kill you, and steal from you. I remember a very vulnerable time in my life where I was asked to come to the bedside of my mom's murderer and pray for him. I didn't think I could do it, but with Christ, I can do all things. And I did.

THE TABLE OF PLENTY

God met me in a dream on November 14, 2019. While at work, I had said to the Lord, "Burn this flesh away, God take out of me what's not like you." In this dream, I was standing by a table with plenty of options to choose from. God began to walk me over to this huge cast iron pot and before I could even open up my mouth, the things that I needed for Him to burn off of me began to burn off.

The Lord then walked back to the table. I followed Him and He invited me to sit down. I said to Him, "Lord I am unworthy. I can't sit with you. I'm unclean." I continued to tell Him everything that was wrong with me...as if He didn't already know my issues. He said, "Daughter, come sup with me. I've prepared this table for you with all this food." As I looked at the table, it was filled with words. These words were, "wisdom, knowledge, understanding, healed, deliverance, salvation, restoration," just to name a few. He said, "Anything that you need is on this table as long as you continue to sup with me." Those things will naturally fall off, my daughter, but keep supping and stay connected to ME. Continue to re-introduce yourself and remember who you are in Me and who I am in you. You will be able to do all things."

THE VISION CAME TOGETHER

In February 2018, God showed me briefly in a dream that I was hosting a Women's Conference, and I was on a stage hosting. I didn't think too much about it. Then in January 2019, I ended up having the same sort of dream about me hosting a conference again. I dreamed that this time the title it was given was *No Wife's Left Behind* and I ended up telling my Pastor about it and He said "If God showed it to you, He will provide everything that you need." I called one of my Sisters who lived in Indianapolis at the time and shared my dream. She also said "Sister," I had a similar dream, this has got to mean something.

On November 14, 2019, I had another dream in which Jesus began to tell me to come sup with Him. He had invited me to a bonfire.

He said, "Daughter, would you come to the sup with me? I am preparing this table for you; it is food, wisdom, knowledge, peace, healing, on the table. It was like a buffet. He said anything that you need is on this table and you can eat anything on this table. He kept saying, "You are welcome to come eat with me, Daughter. Come feast. My words are on this table,"

This meant that His words from the Bible were on the table. He said "All you have to do is come sup with me and receive these things. It's yours." Then we got up from the table and went over to a campfire shaped like a big black kettle. Jesus said to me, "There are things peeling off of you right now." And even before I could open up my mouth, these things were falling off of me. He said, "I have to burn these things off of you so that I can use you, but in the meantime continue to sup with me."

NEW YEARS EVE 2020

God showed me the "Re-Introduce Yourself" Women's Revival and told me to do it. He reminded me that everything that I needed was on the table. All I had to do was sup with Him and He would supply all my needs. He showed me how to remain humble and to trust in Him. An evangelist friend of mine encouraged me to write down everything that I needed for this conference from the budget, speakers, food, venue, and decorations- anything that I needed for God to provide.

I did and God gave me everything that I needed and more! In preparation for the Revival, I had some battles. I knew that these battles would come because I was doing work for the Kingdom. When we stay under the teaching of God and stay connected to Him, He will give us everything we need. God began to show me who my speakers were. I prayed for the location and all logistics. The Revival was a success! People were healed, delivered, and set free. Everything went according to how God wanted it. I was blessed to have my family, friends, and my sisters in the building. I thank God for being who He is.

LET ME RE-INTRODUCE MYSELF

I am a mother. I am a sister. I am a Christian Life Coach. I am a Mentor. I am a friend. I am Evangelist Kenyatta. I am more than a conqueror. *"I can do all things through Christ, who strengthens me" (Philippians 4:13).*

ABOUT THE AUTHOR

Kenyatta P. Hardaway was born and raised in Chicago, Illinois. She a mother, grandmother, an author, mentor, and the Founder and President of *Behind The Veil Christian Life Coaching.*

Kenyatta has an Associate's degree in Child Development from St Paul College Minnesota. In 2018, she received her Diploma in Christian Life Coaching from Liberty University through the American Association of Christian Counseling.

Kenyatta serves her community as a client advocate with the Guiding Star Project, which is a non-profit organization in Minnesota. She is a partner of the Ark of Love & Faith Ministry where she serves in the office of an evangelist. Kenyatta currently resides In Minnesota with her three children and her grandson.

FOLLOW & SUPPORT KENYATTA

Facebook- @ kenyatta.hardaway1

Instagram- @Re-IntroduceYourself

Podcast: anchor.fm/reintroduceyourelf

Website: behindtheveil.simplybook.me

Email: kenyattahardaway@gmail.com

You can connect with Kenyatta in her private Facebook group *Re-Introduce Yourself (Who are you in Christ).*

Re-Introduce Yourself Mini-Journal

Use the following pages to remind yourself who you are in Christ and what you were called to do. Find a quiet space pray and seek God as you move from the past to present and onwards to your future.

My Identity

My name is _____

And I_____

_____

_____

_____

_____

_____

My Life's Scripture

The Scripture that resonates with my life the

most is_____

_____

_____

_____

_____

_____

_____

_____

_____

_____

My Testimony

My Purpose

I was created to_____

_____

_____

_____

_____

_____

_____

_____

My Plan

Short Term Goals (6mos-1year)

1._____

2._____

3._____

Long Term Goals (2-5years)

1._____

2._____

3._____

My Prayer

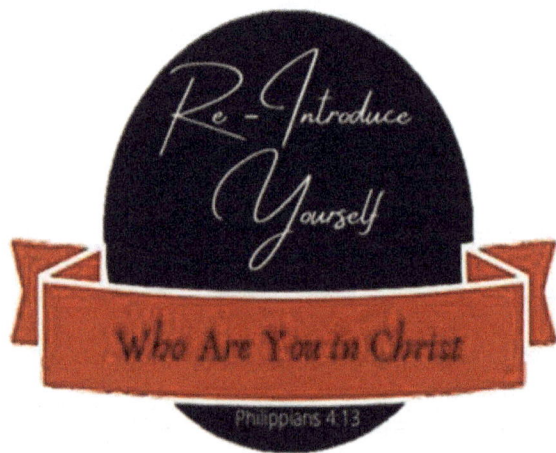

Re - Introduce
Yourself

Who Are You in Christ

Philippians 4:13

Made in the USA
Monee, IL
31 January 2023